CU00994557

Other titles in the series:
The Crazy World of Aerobics (Bill Stott)
The Crazy World of Cats (Bill Stott)
The Crazy World of Cricket (Bill Stott)
The Crazy World of Gardening (Bill Stott)
The Crazy World of Golf (Mike Scott)
The Crazy World of Hospitals (Bill Stott)
The Crazy World of Housework (Bill Stott)
The Crazy World of Learning to Drive (Bill Stott)
The Crazy World of Love (Roland Fiddy)
The Crazy World of Marriage (Bill Stott)
The Crazy World of the Office (Bill Stott)
The Crazy World of Photography (Bill Stott)
The Crazy World of Rugby (Bill Stott)
The Crazy World of Sailing (Peter Rigby)
The Crazy World of Sex (David Pye)
The Crazy World of Soccer (Bill Stott)

This paperback edition published simultaneously in 1992 by Exley
Publications Ltd. in Great Britain, and Exley Giftbooks in the USA.
First hardback edition published in Great Britain in 1988 by Exley
Publications Ltd.

12 11 10 9 8 7 6 5

Copyright © Roland Fiddy, 1988

ISBN 1-85015-344-2

A copy of the CIP data is available from the
British Library on request.

All rights reserved. No part of this publication may be reproduced
or transmitted in any form or by any means, electronic or
mechanical, including photocopy, recording or any information storage
and retrieval system, without permission in writing from
the Publisher.

Printed in Spain by Grafo S.A., Bilbao.

Exley Publications Ltd, 16 Chalk Hill, Watford, Herts WD1 4BN,
United Kingdom.
Exley Giftbooks, 232 Madison Avenue, Suite 1206, NY 10016, USA.

"*For goodness sake don't admire his fretwork – he might give us something!*"

①

BANG!

②

"You were lucky – the paint pot broke your fall!"

"You might as well go back to George - your father is redecorating too!"

1.

2.

Even the most efficient 'Do-It-Yourselfers' ...

QUICK DRYING PAINT

3.

… get stuck from time to time.

"Not to worry – I'll paint that later."

1.

2.

3.

4.

Whether you are decorating a living room or tiling a bathroom, make sure you see eye to eye with your partner.

"It's the garden shed self-assembly kit we ordered!"

"Well, have you managed to stop the picture jumping, dear?"

Unfortunately, do-it-yourselfers have to …

... live with their mistakes.

"So far so good!"

"I like it, except I <u>hate</u> green!"

"Stop asking stupid questions and call a mechanic!"

"I think I've found the trouble, Arthur!"

1.

2.

3.

Do-it-yourselfers should always be willing …

... to listen to informed advice.

I.

People may think a job is beyond your capabilities ...

... *surprise them!*

"I'm calling about the electric drill you sold my husband."

"Those eyes follow me around, and it isn't even switched on!"

"Bernard never gives up on a job ... but you don't want to hear my troubles."

1.

2.

"Remind me, Doris – how many days off have I got left?"

"Don't hurry me! A rushed job is a botched job"

1.

2.

3.

4.

5.

"*I'm sorry, Bert – it was either drop the can or have an accident.*"

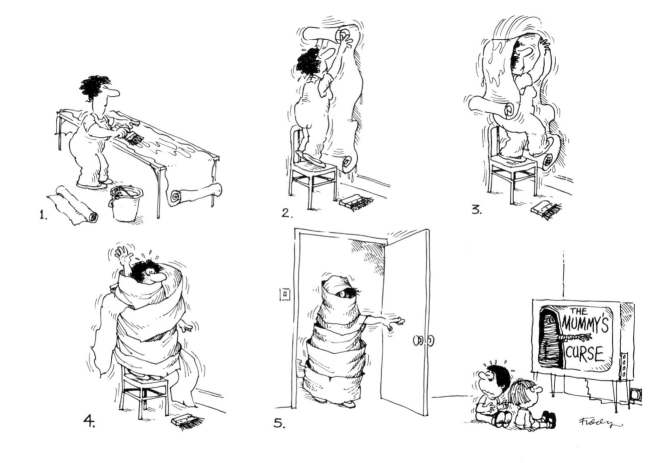

1.

2.

3.

4.

5.

THE MUMMY'S CURSE

Beware of the deadly bite of the cantilever toolbox.

"I'm ready to say to hell with it if you are!"

Teamwork is the key to successful decorating.

"Help!"

Unfortunately, enthusiastic handymen ...

2

... do not always receive ...

3.

... the appreciation they deserve.

"You should go up again immediately or you'll lose your nerve!"

"I think it's your way of getting away from it all!"

"Stop moaning! The doctor said you needed outside interests!"

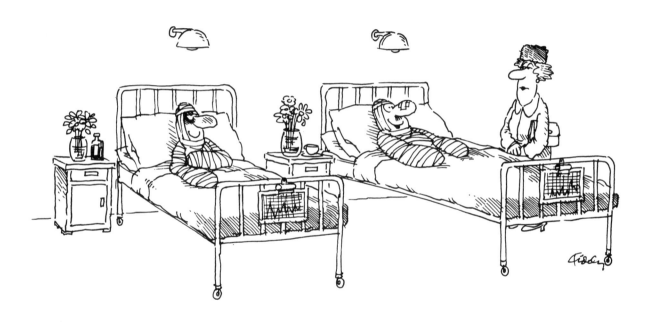

"Talk about coincidences – Malcolm here is a decorating fanatic too!"

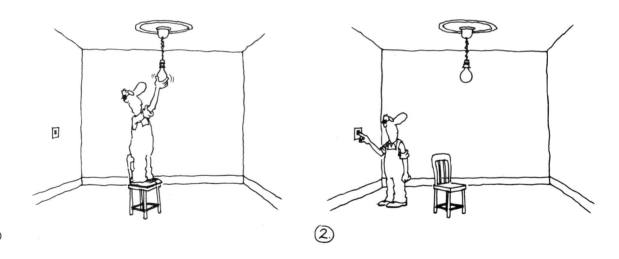

③

④

"How's it going, Michelangelo?"

"Is that the florists? Please send round another indoor plant!"

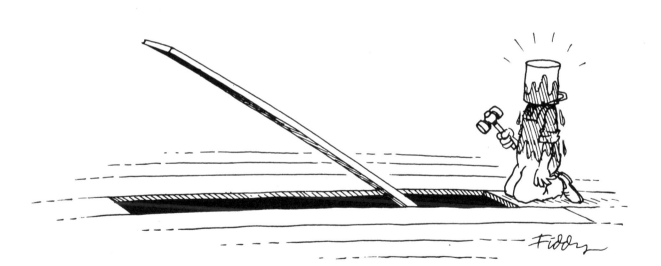

"No thanks – I'm just browsing."

"We've chosen a lovely restful green for the walls."

"Well, I don't think you've read it at all!"

"His enthusiasm is infectious!"

Books in the "Crazy World" series

($4.99 £2.99 paperback)

The Crazy World of Aerobics (Bill Stott)
The Crazy World of Cats (Bill Stott)
The Crazy World of Cricket (Bill Stott)
The Crazy World of Gardening (Bill Stott)
The Crazy World of Golf (Mike Scott)
The Crazy World of The Handyman (Roland Fiddy)
The Crazy World of Hospitals (Bill Stott)
The Crazy World of Housework (Bill Stott)
The Crazy World of Learning to Drive (Bill Stott)
The Crazy World of Love (Roland Fiddy)
The Crazy World of Marriage (Bill Stott)
The Crazy World of The Office (Bill Stott)
The Crazy World of Photography (Bill Stott)
The Crazy World of Rugby (Bill Stott)
The Crazy World of Sailing (Peter Rigby)
The Crazy World of Sex (David Pye)
The Crazy World of Soccer (Bill Stott)

Books in the "Mini Joke Book" series

($6.99 £3.99 hardback)

These attractive 64 page mini joke books are illustrated throughout by Bill Stott.

A Binge of Diet Jokes
A Bouquet of Wedding Jokes
A Feast of After Dinner Jokes
A Knockout of Sports Jokes
A Portfolio of Business Jokes
A Round of Golf Jokes
A Romp of Naughty Jokes
A Spread of Over-40s Jokes
A Tankful of Motoring Jokes
A Triumph of Over-50s Jokes

Books in the "Fanatics" series

($4.99 £2.99 paperback)

The **Fanatic's Guides** are perfect presents for everyone with a hobby that has got out of hand. Eighty pages of hilarious black and white cartoons by Roland Fiddy.

The Fanatic's Guide to the Bed
The Fanatic's Guide to Cats
The Fanatic's Guide to Computers
The Fanatic's Guide to Dads
The Fanatic's Guide to Diets
The Fanatic's Guide to Dogs
The Fanatic's Guide to Golf
The Fanatic's Guide to Husbands
The Fanatic's Guide to Money
The Fanatic's Guide to Sex
The Fanatic's Guide to Skiing
The Fanatic's Guide to Sports

Books in the "Victim's Guide" series

($4.99 £2.99 paperback)

Award winning cartoonist Roland Fiddy sees the funny side to life's phobias, nightmares and catastrophes.

The Victim's Guide to Air Travel
The Victim's Guide to the Baby
The Victim's Guide to the Christmas
The Victim's Guide to the Dentist
The Victim's Guide to the Doctor
The Victim's Guide to Middle Age

Great Britain: Order these super books from your local bookseller or from Exley Publications Ltd, 16 Chalk Hill, Watford, Herts WD1 4BN. (Please send £1.30 to cover postage and packing on 1 book, £2.60 on 2 or more books.)